CW01583078

This book belongs to:

____

____

____

____

SILHOUETTES

MACHINES

Illustrated by Maureen Galvani

Here is a...

tractor to help

on the farm.

Here is a...

in the street.

Here is a...

Here is a...

us to town.

Here is a...

for petrol.

Here is an…

And here is a...

us on holiday.

And here is a...